MW01098444

Un-Bias Guide for Leaders:

Unconscious Bias & Conscious Choices

By Deborah J. Levine

UN-BIAS GUIDE SERIES

MATRIX MODEL

MANAGEMENT SYSTEM

Books by Deborah J. Levine

The Liberator's Daughter

Matrix Model Management System:
Guide to Cross Cultural Wisdom

Inspire your Inner Global Leader:
True Stories for New Leaders

Going Southern:
The No-Mess Guide to Success in the South

STEM Women Study Guide

Teaching Curious Christians about Judaism

Bunny Bear Audio CD
Adventures in Diversity Land

Religious Diversity at Work:
Guide to Religious Diversity in US Workplace

Religious Diversity in our Schools

Write That Book; Tell That Story
The Magic Marble Tree (release date: 2019)

Published by Deborah Levine Enterprises, LLC

Chattanooga, TN 37412

1 (423) 805-4602

© Deborah Levine 2018 ...

E-mail: info@diversityreport.com

Web: www.americandiversityreport.com

TABLE OF CONTENTS

INTRODUCTION: The Un-Bias Matrix System

You've heard of technology companies receiving diversity awards when their executive suite is almost entirely white and male. You've heard how interviewers reading the same resume with different names choose the one with a name that sounds like their own. It doesn't surprise you that firms looking for computer geeks hire millennials over boomers. Organizations that value diversity but with cafeterias that look segregated according to race and gender aren't a surprise either. Nor is the team that sits in sullen silence in a diversity training designed to overcome bias. Some are thinking, "I have no biases, unconscious or conscious." Others are thinking, "It's hopeless. Why bother?"

Turn on the news, open a newspaper, or check what's trending online and you'll see that unconscious bias is a major issue in the workplace, education, and politics. Yet, despite the intensified focus, defining unconscious bias is not a simple task. One of the best definitions comes from Marc Brenman, Managing Partner, IDARE LLL

> "An inclination that influences judgment. A disposition exerting a distorting influence on judgment. The influence can be characterized as distorting in that it leads to a judgment which departs from the norms of rationality. The term may be used in a descriptive way to mean an inclination, but more often is used as a term of evaluation to mean an inclination that influences judgment and ought not to. Prejudice is a synonym for bias in this pejorative sense. However, bias cannot be completely eliminated, in contrast to prejudice that can and should be eliminated."

How can we deal with this complex, under-the-radar phenomenon? The workplace, organization, and community already struggle with prejudice, or conscious bias that leads to discrimination. Can the underlying unconscious biases be addressed at the same time? Or is the neuroscience science behind it too complex?

The complex brain activity underlying bias, along with the emotional potential, is illustrated in an article in *Psychology Today* by Dr. Bernard J. Luskin.
(https://www.psychologytoday.com/us/blog/the-media-psychology-effect/201604/mris-reveal-unconscious-bias-in-the-brain)

> "… neuroimaging shows that decision-making automatically triggers specific regions of the brain responsible for unconscious processing, including those measured by the Implicit Association Test. MRI imaging showing which regions of the brain are activated during biased responses allow us, i.e., you, to see the occurrence of biased associations … The amygdala is an almond-shaped set of neurons deep in the temporal lobe. The amygdala has emerged as a key region of the brain in MRI bias research. The amygdala is the "emotional" center of the brain that reacts to fear and threat and other senses. Scientists have found a measurable correlation between amygdala activity and implicit racial bias. The point again is that research shows a visual brain response, even though an individual may not be conscious of it."

While most of us are not neuroscientists looking at MRIs and seeing the brain activity around biases, we do see the effects of unconscious biases, prejudice, and discrimination. How can we not address both the intentional and unintentional thought processes? The key is to find ways to do so that are both useful to non-scientists and respectful of the neuroscience nuances. A valuable and carefully balanced perspective comes from Dr. Carlos Cortes, Professor Emeritus of the History Dept. of the University of California at Riverside. Dr. Cortes asserts that conscious thought includes decision-making, helps with empathy, considers multiple perspectives, and allows us to think about our own thinking. Dr. Cortes defines unconscious thought as a process that categorizes, reduces complexities, makes connections, and creates coherent stories from disparate facts.

The Un-Bias Matrix does not intend to be a scientific thesis. Instead, it is based on three decades of field testing data structuring, storytelling methodology, and conscious choice strategies with teams and their leaders. Note: References to neuro-pathways, their connections, and the integration of new thought patterns are intended to be populist interpretations of highly complex neuroscience, not as a substitute for the neuroscience.

The Un-Bias Matrix process is a cultural anthropology-based approach to training leaders and teams. I'm deeply grateful for my early training in the cultural anthropology of Claude Levi Strauss, which has left me with some unconscious biases that have been helpful in the organization, structuring, and articulation of complex human thought processes in our tumultuous times. To meet the challenge of managing discriminatory unconscious bias, I have combined Levi Strauss with my background in Urban Planning. The result is a training template I call the 4-Step Un-Bias Matrix System:

1. AWARENESS: Communication

Create the mental infrastructure to sharpen listening skills, process the Big Data of diverse cultures, and begin communicating across cultural boundaries.

2. SENSITIVITY: Emotion

Create the emotional intelligence to assess comfort levels, anticipate potential conflicts, and manage ongoing clashes. Develop a common language and metrics for emotional responses and minimize biases that interfere with collaborative efforts.

3. COMPETENCE: Wisdom

Combine growing AWARENESS and SENSITIVITY with problem-solving skills to increase the capacity for building wise decision-making skills; develop short and long-term plans for carrying out the vision.

4. PLANNING: Mission & Policies

Apply the AWARENESS, SENSITIVITY, and COMPETENCE sections to make conscious choices in planning for the future. You, your team, and your workplace can help shape policies and procedures that reflect your mission of Un-Bias.

SECTION 1: The Unconscious Bias Challenge

"We tend to accept information that confirms our prior beliefs and ignore or discredit information that does not. This confirmation bias settles over our eyes like distorting spectacles for everything we look at."
~ Kyle Hill, Science Writer

What we know, or think we know, has been the target of philosophers and scientists throughout time. The challenge of overcoming biases is captured in centuries of memorable quotes by philosophers, economists, and scientists. Some have posed the issue as ignorance. "Real knowledge is to know the extent of one's ignorance," ~ Confucius (551-479 BCE). While the term "ignorance" remains popular, we are increasingly looking to science to explain the phenomenon of our mindset.

Today, we are exploring learned thought patterns through scientific means and understand that they are easily activated and difficult to disconnect. Research means increased familiarity with the complexity of these thought patterns, but doesn't necessarily make them easier to address. The lack of awareness implicit in unconscious thought patterns and biases presents a powerful challenge to restructuring them. The challenge is not a new one and there are no instant solutions.

"The difficulty lies, not in the new ideas, but in escaping the old ones, which ramify, for those brought up as most of us have been, into every corner of our minds."
~ John Maynard Keynes, Economist (1883-1946)

Our struggle to comprehend and integrate knowledge and new ideas is intensified in our current divisive world. Unconscious bias is a factor in that divisiveness that leads to discrimination in our communities, workplaces, and social institutions. However, unconscious bias should not be identified as hate. True hate is bone deep, mind numbing, and civilization destroying. Groups that promote hate consciously add to the hostility and violence towards those who are different. Whether the Other refers to race, ethnicity, nationality, or religion, hate doesn't stop at discrimination. The Other is considered a threat to be eliminated.

Hate groups are often an issue for law enforcement, rather than a subject for cross-cultural and diversity training. The language of hate may unleash and intensify unconscious biases, so that they merge with hate, and for some, the distinction may seem irrelevant. But unless activated at the level of hate, unconscious bias remains in the interpersonal arena. Understanding that emotions can ramp up biases, organization policies should be designed to control and set boundaries for language and behavior.

To address unconscious bias effectively, each individual needs to be aware of and articulate how the diverse elements in their lives and backgrounds connect. This is done through the Communication Matrix. Second, each individual needs to develop a sensitivity to the emotional component of this process. Teams can also acquire that sensitivity through shared terminology and metrics, enabling better management of emotional clashes. This is done through the Emotion Matrix. Third, individuals need to internalize a system for problem-solving that is evidence-based, equitable, sustainable, and accountable, and which is also applicable in a team setting. This is achieved with the Wisdom Matrix. Lastly, teams can use the Mission Matrix to plan programs that boost fairness and trust within organizations and with served populations.

Let us understand the magnitude of moving from unconscious bias to non-discriminating choices. It's not a matter of simply being aware of workplace diversity. Research has shown that forcing a team into awareness of cultural differences can often add stress to relationships and defensiveness to communication. Further, labeling people as racist and sexist seldom enhances their desire to be inclusive and respectful. This was dramatically demonstrated in the case of a Google engineer who rejected the training as "shaming" and insisted that women are biologically unsuited to technical computer work. Rather than bludgeoning people, there needs to be a more -effective, nuanced, and humane approach.

Managing unconscious bias requires the development of new neuro-pathways and building new connections to and within those pathways. Children are able to engage in this process as part of growing up. You can see the phenomenon if you move your family to a new country, as mine did when I was in elementary school. It's a natural way to build the ability to travel between worlds and adjust to cultural differences while maintaining your core identity. If this experience has not been yours, you may have to work harder to achieve the same results. But you can find a path to building neuro-pathways and restructuring their connections, and the Un-Bias Matrix puts you on that path.

If a corporation is the context, think of the corporate culture's neuro system as its recruitment, hiring, and promotion policies. The interviews, performance reviews, customer service training, and mentorship programs are neuro-pathways in the system's decision-making. Training should be customized for each department while building a common language and metrics for all departments across the organization.

Given its complexity, Un-Bias Matrix training should be ongoing rather than a one-time event. Each training event should be focused on the development and integration of the Communication Matrix and Emotion Matrix and then proceed to the Wisdom and Mission Matrices. Awareness and sensitivity are then combined with the elements of wise decision-making: knowledge, character, and vision with the elements of planning: goals, objectives, and tasks. Periodic training and coaching solidify the connections and foster the team's growing competence. Involvement by the executive team, especially if they are role models in the process, maximizes the competence of the entire organization. A corporate culture can be transformed by an executive team that reflects the Un-Bias Matrix approach in its own makeup and in polices/procedures/practices, targeted outreach, nondiscrimination, equal employment opportunity, handling complaints, and dispute resolution.

If the community is the context, consider the neuro-pathways to be the societal structures, including education, economics, and politics. A systematic approach to managing the detrimental effects of unconscious bias in each case helps manage emotional clashes that might otherwise intensify. The first in the series of the Matrix Model Management System was a Guide to Cross-cultural Wisdom. It reflected the methodology of cultural anthropology and was designed to address the challenges of rapid globalization in relatively isolated areas.

The Matrix System was originally applied to a community in the western suburbs of Chicago, where international companies were rapidly globalizing the region. The culture clashes that erupted were primarily around the issue of religion and religious expression in the schools. The Matrix System was used to interact with the community, its business sector, law enforcement, and the public school system. The result was workshops, presentations, and Matrix-like Quick Reference Religious Diversity Cards in books such as *Religious Diversity in Our Schools* and *Religious Diversity at Work*.

Ten years ago, the Matrix System was used for community-wide Global Leadership Class and a Youth Global Leadership Class in Chattanooga, Tennessee. With training sessions based on the Matrix System, Chattanooga community leaders acquired a global mindset to better interact with the growing number of international companies in the area. Volkswagen, in particular, looked for that mindset in its hiring and promoting practices.

The Matrix Model Management System: Guide to Cross-cultural Wisdom System was formalized in a textbook and accompanying workbook. The flexibility and applicability of the Matrix System has meant its incorporation into the training programs of multiple sectors, including government agencies, healthcare organizations, education institutions, nonprofits, and corporations. The *Un-Bias Guide for Leaders* is part of the Matrix System's Un-Bias Guide Series and is customized specifically for leaders and teams in the workplace. The companion book, *Un-Bias Guide for Educators* is designed for schools and the classroom.

Both books in the Un-Bias Guide Series begin with an exercise that highlights our different perceptions of diversity, starting us on the path to awareness of unconscious bias.

INTRODUCTORY MATRIX EXERCISE

Ask the workshop participants to look around the room and consider the question: How diverse is this room? Give the group metrics for measuring that diversity based on 1 (extremely), 2 (moderately), 3 (somewhat), or 4 (not much).

After 2-3 minutes, explain that you will call out the numbers one at a time. Each participant should raise their hand when the number is called that they chose. Going through the process will demonstrate that although everyone is sitting in the same room with the same participants, the perception of the diversity of those participants will vary.

Ask for volunteers to explain their responses. The explanations will help the volunteers be aware of the diversity categories that matter most to them. Their explanations will also help the participants be aware of how others process differences.

The workshop leader then asks all participants to brainstorm a list of all diversity categories and have that list written where are participants can see it.

SECTION 2: The Culture Awareness Map

"Without the discovery of uniformities there can be no concepts, no classifications, no formulations, no principles, no laws; and without these no science can exist."
~Clyde Kluckhohn, cultural anthropologist (1905-1960)

The Matrix System is intended for workshops, ideally for a large group with breakout sessions of 4-6 people around tables within the larger room/group. It begins with a uniform structure that can be universally applicable: the Culture Awareness Map, as per Dr. Carlos Cortes' definition of unconscious thought as a process that categorizes, reduces complexities, makes connections, and creates coherent stories from disparate facts. Therefore, the Un-Bias Matrix begins with a map for simplifying the Big Data of cultural differences, beginning with the cultural expressions.

The structure of the Culture Awareness Map is a triangle with its three points representing our personal backgrounds: Geography/History, Family/Diversity, and Beliefs/Style. Geography refers to traits shaped by the place(s) where we grew up and the impact of its history. Family/Diversity refers to the population that influenced us and our inherited diversity.

Our Beliefs/Style refers to our values and personality. Although we have this category in common, there is substantial diversity of thought, given our personal blend of Geography/History and Demographics/Diversity. The variations are virtually infinite when we add universal themes in the structure of society, including Education, Economics, Politics, and Religion. It's not surprising that our brains use shortcuts to manage this Big Data.

Shortcuts are cultural expressions that capture huge amounts of data in compact packages. Unconscious biases are often triggered by cultural expressions such as music, architecture, symbols, and sports. They can capture your culture map and your story in a single detail, so remember that every detail counts.

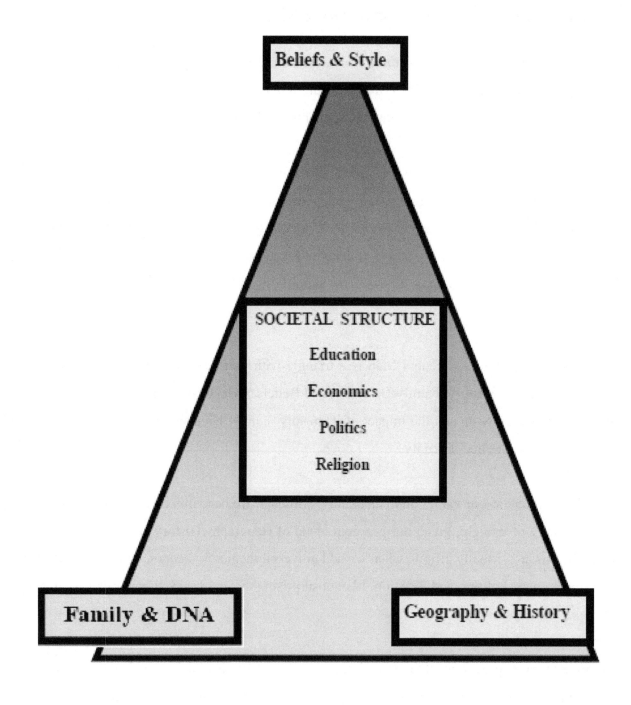

CULTURE MAP OPTIONS

GEOGRAPHY CATEGORY
The context of Geography can be made at different levels according to size:

• Site

• Neighborhood

• City

• State

• County

• Region

• Country

HISTORY CATEGORY

The History context can be made using references to historical figures, activities, and trends:

• Influential people

• Business and industries

• Political happenings

FAMILY CATEGORY

The Family category includes generational elements that have shaped our individual backgrounds:

• Immigrant origins

• Education levels

• Professions

• Political influences

• Religious affiliations

DNA CATEGORY

The DNA category refers to our diversity elements that are inherited and/or physical:

• Gender

• Race

• Ethnicity

- Gender Orientation
- Disabilities
- Other physical characteristics including size

BELIEFS CATEGORY

Our Belief systems may center on religion but also has a variety of elements as noted below:

- Values
- Ethics
- Hope
- Optimism
- Pessimism
- Ideals
- Faith
- Humane

STYLE CATEGORY

Our verbal and nonverbal styles of communication have many possible combinations. Here are four common groupings: 1) Dominant, 2) Competent 3) Diplomatic and 4) Under-the-Radar.

Dominant

- Verbal Style: direct
- Tone of Voice: authoritarian, loud
- Body Language: intense eye contact, emphatic hand gestures, stern face, tense posture

Competent

- Verbal Style: direct
- Tone of Voice: authoritative, moderate loudness, fast, moderate monotone
- Body Language: upright relaxed posture, moderate eye contact, neutral facial expression

Diplomatic

- Verbal Style: indirect, formal
- Tone of voice: moderate softness, slow/smooth, questioning
- Body Language: relaxed posture, leaning toward listener, friendly smile, moderate eye contact

Under-the-Radar

- Verbal Style: indirect

- Tone of voice: soft, slow, hesitant

- Body Language: slumped posture, minimal eye contact, neutral facial expression

CULTURE AWARENESS MAP - EXERCISE #1

DEFINE YOURSELF: Participants develop understanding of their cultural similarities and differences using the Cultural Map. Referencing the three points of the map's triangle in the following questions prompts a multi-dimensional awareness of themselves and others. Note that writing often prompts the conscious brain to become actively engaged in articulating our unconscious thoughts.

A.   Where did you grow up? (Geography)

B.   Name a famous person of that Geography. (History)

C.   How many generations has your family been in America? (Family)

D.   Name an inherited or physical category that represents you. (DNA)

E.   Are you an optimist or a pessimist about the future? (Beliefs)

F.   How would you describe your usual tone of voice? (Style)

CULTURE AWARENESS MAP - EXERCISE #2

Objective: Participants will compare and contrast how geography, history, and family affect their perception of others and the ways in which they connect using descriptive key words.

AWARENESS: To better understand that we all have unconscious biases, answer these questions by circling your reaction: 1 = Love, 2 = Like, 3 = Dislike, 4 = Dismiss. Next, describe which points on the triangle are related to your reaction in order to increase conscious awareness.

When I hear a salesperson speak with the accent I heard growing up, my reaction is ...

1 = Love   2 = Like   3 = Dislike   4 = Dismiss

Relevant Map Points _____

When I interview someone who has the same last name as I do, my reaction is ...

1 = Love   2 = Like   3 = Dislike   4 = Dismiss

Relevant Map Points _____

When a new employee shakes my hand energetically, my reaction is ...

1 = Love   2 = Like   3 = Dislike   4 = Dismiss

Relevant Map Points _____

When a colleague speaks clearly and loudly, my reaction is ...

1 = Love   2 = Like   3 = Dislike   4 = Dismiss

Relevant Map Points _____

When a stranger on the street smiles at me, my reaction is ...

1 = Love   2 = Like   3 = Dislike   4 = Dismiss

Relevant Map Points _____

SECTION 3: The Communication Matrix

"Words are singularly the most powerful force available to humanity. We can choose to use this force constructively with words of encouragement, or destructively using words of despair. Words have energy and power with the ability to help, to heal, to hinder, to hurt, to harm, to humiliate and to humble."

~ Yehuda Berg

The COMMUNICATION MATRIX expands the Map by transforming the unconscious connections we weave into stories into more conscious, thoughtful storytelling. Storytelling is an ancient form of communication common to virtually every culture on the planet because of its ability to capture large amounts of data in compact packages. Whether ancient myths, the Bible, or movies today, the art of storytelling has shaped our thinking, beliefs, and cultures. For the cultural anthropologist, the art of storytelling is also a science.

When Harvard established the first university major of Folklore & Mythology in the context of Cultural Anthropology in the 1960s, the field was considered esoteric and it attracted few students. Yet, several of its graduates worked for the military during the Vietnam War to decode the culture to better anticipate local reactions. The origin of the COMMUNICATION MATRIX is similar to the science that of these graduates. It uses the traditional categories of reporting: Who, What, When, Where, and Why. But it also blends iconic cultural expressions as cultural shorthand into that combination to boost conscious and unconscious communication across cultural boundaries. Each individual now proceeds to contract their own story.

1. WHO

We begin our story with the "Who" column. Who is speaking? Who is the main action figure? For the greatest impact on unconscious bias, the answer to that question is either you or another individual, rather than an impersonal group. When you add a category or categories of diversity, you will be addressing the issue of bias. Whether it is generational differences, gender, race, ethnicity, religion, the diversity category, or categories, your choices dictate the plot development.

What about the "Whom"? This is the subject of the story; the person or group on the receiving end of the communication. When we define the "Whom," we begin to define the moral of our story. Your Who & Whom choices set the scene and the story begins to unfold.

2. WHAT

The next theme in our Un-Bias Matrix is the "What." This is the trigger for the story. The trigger launches the story's plot with an incident, a disagreement, a stalemate, or some kind of dilemma. Regardless of the nature of the trigger, it should relate to the unconscious bias that you want to enlighten. For example, if you want to address racism, you might choose for your "What" the incident at Starbucks when two young African American men were arrested for trespassing while waiting for a friend. Your story then builds on the incident, adding context details with "When" and "Where."

3. WHEN

Time is a necessary element for the relevancy of our stories because it provides a quick connection to unconscious thinking. The calendar is a ready-made categorization tool that can moves the brain quickly into the time dimension of a religious holy day, national celebration, or seasonal reference. Your audience can immediately resonate to the timing if you choose a holiday that resonates with your Who & Whom. However, if you choose a holiday that is unfamiliar or not relevant, that unconscious connection will not happen. For example, setting your story on July 4 for an audience that is British and unlikely to relate to America's Independence Day will lose its intended impact.

Note that timing doesn't necessarily refer to the calendar. Your story can reference a specific hour in the day, day of the week, or month of the year. The brain quickly begins to assign meaning and personal memories to the timing. For example, consider the different reactions to a story that takes place at 2:00 am, as opposed to a story that begins at noon.

4. WHERE

The "Where" describes our geographic context and can range from a city to a classroom. Each story plays out differently, depending on its context. Effective communication matches the context to the story. Clarity of "Where" leads to clarity of context without which the story becomes more difficult to process and has less impact. The context will also determine the style of the story, particularly the level of formality you use to tell it.

5. WHY

The Un-Bias Matrix provides two approaches for explaining the "Why." The first method involves facts: science, logic, and proof. The second method involves beliefs. Facts educate while beliefs motivate. Story-telling can embrace both.

"I want to be part of the storytelling that educates people and awakens a sense of compassion in other people of the kind of people they don't encounter in their daily lives very frequently."

~ Kelly McCreary

CULTURAL SHORTHAND

Communication can be made more powerful with the use of its cultural shorthand, which can range from idioms and slang to iconic movies, sports, food, art, and monuments. The Matrix System borrows from cultural anthropology and uses the term "artifacts" to describe these cultural expressions. When embedded in stories, artifacts are powerful tools to interact with unconscious bias. When the artifacts resonate, they create powerful connections that can either create inspiration or aversion.

To demonstrate the power of artifacts, consider the example of a Mother's Day card. If the card depicts multiple Caucasian women and you send it to an African American friend, your disconnect with the diversity aspect of the woman to whom you send it may short-circuit your good intentions. The lack of awareness is a lack of connection that a story can help correct.

"Cognitive psychology has shown that the mind best understands facts when they are woven into a conceptual fabric, such as a narrative, mental map, or intuitive theory. Disconnected facts in the mind are like unlinked pages on the Web:

They might as well not exist."

~ Steven Pinker

COMMUNICATION UN-BIAS MATRIX					
WHO	WHAT	WHEN	WHERE	WHY	SHORT HAND
Gender	Incident	Holy Day	Office	Faith	Movies
Race	Stale mate	Holiday	Street	Hope	TV
Ethnicity	Conflict	Night Time	Home	Equity	Music
Age	Clash	Daytime	Group	Kind	Food
Religion	Shun	Yearly	Class room	Facts	Art
Region	Insult	Monthly	Airport	Logic	Symbols
Socio-Economic	Mistake	Weekly	Store	Training	Names

COMMUNICATION MATRIX WORKSHEETS

Objective: Participants will organize and analyze data about themselves using cultural shorthand to synthesize data.

The worksheets can be used to introduce workshops and other training events that build diverse teams and address unconscious bias. They can also be used as ice breakers and introductions. Filling out these sheets provides information about the participants to the attendees. The process of writing the responses is an exercise in consciously organizing background information. Organizing data for an audience rather than for personal, internal use is a valuable element in transforming unconscious thinking into conscious thought.

Many of the worksheets begin with shorthand items and use the exercise to unpack information compacted within them. The process involves re-thinking, re-organizing, and re-structuring thought patterns. Strategies for using the results include the following:

- Each individual reads their worksheet story to the whole group.
- Each individual reads their story to a smaller break-out group.
- Results can be compiled either by full set of answers or by specific answers.
- Answers can be written on index cards and displayed on storyboards/walls.
- Results can be used to divide the group into teams based on specific answers.
- The trainer can share an analysis of the results.

We begin with the Names worksheet used for introductions and ice breakers at training workshops. Note the sample responses and assessment that follow the worksheet.

WORKSHEET 1: NAMES

Names are cultural shorthand and dense information carriers. They are windows into personalities, cultures, and values. By answering these simple questions, you will be teaching, sharing, and engaging at new levels:

1.   My full name is:

2.   I was named after:

3.   My parents gave me this name because:

4.   I like/dislike my name because:

5.   My friends call me:

6.   If I ever changed my name I would choose:

SAMPLE RESPONSES TO NAMES

Participant 1

1. My name is Clarence Clark O'Leary.

2. My middle name is a family name since we came to America a century ago from Ireland.

3. My parents named me after the famous lawyer, Clarence Darrow.

4. I dislike my name because it doesn't sound like me.

5. I like my colleagues to call me Clark and I sign my name as C. Clark O'Leary.

6. If I ever changed my name, I would choose Miguel because I like Latin-sounding names.

MATRIX ANALYSIS

The storyteller is male with Irish roots that go back generations. He prefers individuality over tradition. There's a generational change from his parents' choices and an openness to new cultural influences. Note that the sound of names often triggers an unconscious bias, whether negative (doesn't sound like me) or positive (I like Latin-sounding names).

Note: These worksheets should be shared out loud in small breakout groups. In addition, ask for volunteers to share their responses with the larger group. If there are no volunteers, call on a few people and build awareness that leadership involves that visibility.

SAMPLE RESPONSES TO NAMES

Participant 2

1. My name is LaMae O'Hara.

7. My last name came from the family that owned my great great-grandfather when he was still a slave.

8. My parents gave me the name because this was a girlhood friend of my mother.

9. I like my name because it is unique.

10. I like my colleagues to call me LaMae because it sounds like music.

11. I would never change my name because it has family meaning.

MATRIX ANALYSIS

The storyteller is female and African American. She identifies with family that extends back to slave times. While she values individual uniqueness, she is equally invested in family and history. She values the sound of her name, underscoring how unfamiliar names may trigger unconscious bias.

Note: Asking participants to share their likes and dislikes can help bring awareness to unconscious thinking.

WORKSHEET: Shorthand - The "Why"

One of the questions that people struggle with in storytelling is the "Why." When they are asked "Why," they are often unable to articulate their mindset, including values, beliefs, and biases. The cultural icons we admire and the ones we dislike provide a shortcut to that mindset. When we assign well-known figures and other cultural shorthand traits that we either admire or dislike, we build conscious awareness of ourselves. The sequence of questions in this exercise takes us from unconscious to conscious thinking.

"WHY" EXERCISE Part A: Inspirational

1. And icon who I admire is:

2. A character trait that I admire about this person is:

3. A movie or television show that illustrates this trait is:

4. A famous historical or fictional person that illustrates that trait is:

5. Why is this trait necessary in your workplace/classroom/community?

"WHY" EXERCISE Part B - Cautionary

1. A well-known figure who I dislike:

2. A character trait that I dislike about this person is:

3. A movie or television show that illustrates this trait is:

4. A famous historical or fictional person that illustrates that trait is:

5. What impact does this trait have in your workplace/classroom/community?

SAMPLE "WHY" RESPONSES

Part A:

A character trait I admire is loyalty.

A movie that demonstrates loyalty is *A Tale of Two Cities*.

Famous people who showed their loyalty: The Lone Ranger and Tonto.

Loyalty in the workplace means that you can trust your colleagues to work as a team.

Part B:

A character trait the I dislike is lack of loyalty.

A movie that demonstrates a lack of loyalty is *Nine to Five*.

A famous corporation with a lack of loyalty is Enron.

Lack of loyalty in the workplace may mean less stagnation, but it also means more conflicts of interests, less trust, and more political in-fighting.

MATRIX ANALYSIS

While the character trait, loyalty, is the same in both answers, the generational differences of the two respondents are evident in the choice of cultural shorthand. Shortcuts that resonate with the target audience will use unconscious bias positively to emphasize a point. Shortcuts that do not resonate may trigger a negative response.

SECTION 4: The Emotion Matrix

"Whether your role is to lead others or simply to lead yourself, acutely understanding what you are feeling and perceiving is the prerequisite to understanding what others think and feel."
~ Doc Childre and Bruce Cryer (2005)

In a team setting, diversity can lead to creativity and innovation, but it can also generate disagreements, arguments, and disputes. As we come up against each other's biases, whether conscious or unconscious, emotional clashes follow. The results can be resentment and hostility with a decreased capacity to control intensifying emotions. That decrease can lead to adrenaline-fueled knee jerk reactions and have long-term ramifications, including less collaboration. For that reason, there are claims that diversity training is a well-intentioned failure with little positive impact on team dynamics or company policies of hiring, promotion, and non-discrimination.

"Most diversity and inclusion initiatives fall into the former category: sincere ignorance. They look and sound great. They are usually well-meaning too. But a vast number of these initiatives prove ineffective or fail within a year or two. Why? Sincere ignorance: Start talking to the people who put them together, and more often than not you realize that the details and depth of strategic thinking behind them is as thin as the paper they are printed on."
~ Glenn Llopis, *Forbes Magazine* (Jan. 2017) https://www.forbes.com/sites/glennllopis/2017/01/16/5-reasons-diversity-and-inclusion-fails/#7f22944250df

Rather than label the problem as "ignorance," consider the lack of strategic thinking as an unconscious bias problem. Assumptions are made, biases revealed, and when the resulting confrontation is perceived as a threat, the fight-or-flight syndrome is activated. If we can track the intensity of our emotions in the process, we may have the ability and opportunity to consciously choose our response.

THE EMOTION BAROMETER

"If you can't measure it, you can't improve it."
~ Peter Drucker (1909-2005)

We quantify our emotions by creating an Emotion Barometer. The metrics of that barometer begin with the individual and are eventually applied to groups and teams. The barometer designates stages of emotional intensity into four levels plus a transitional level labelled "Disorientation." The use of storytelling to express and quantify each level personalizes the barometer. By defining our emotional levels using stories, we create mental shorthand that names the emotions, giving us more control over them.

The following Emotion Barometer can be used by all individuals in the workplace. The stories following the Emotion Barometer are designed as examples and prompts for your own stories.

The goal of the Emotion Matrix is to apply the storytelling process to teams and enable a group process that manages the emotions involved with dealing with biases. This chapter includes team exercises to accomplish this goal.

EMOTION UN-BIAS MATRIX - Levels			
LEVEL #1	**LEVEL #2**	**LEVEL #3**	**LEVEL #4**
Calm	2nd Choice	Upset	Enraged
Peaceful	Tolerable	Unhappy	Vengeful
Centered	Plan B	Annoyed	Resentful
Pleased	Acceptable	Uncomfortable	Disgusted
IDEAL	**OK**	**UPSET**	**NIGHTMARE**

TRAVELING THROUGH EMOTION LEVELS

We can use stories to show what happens when we travel from an idyllic emotional place to the opposite end of the spectrum, the worst-case scenario. When we name our emotions, they become clearer in our minds. When we identify each with a story, we are well on our way to creating metrics for our emotions. Here are samples of stories that flesh out our 4-level Barometer. Each story will come to mind the next time we're at a similar emotion level, solidifying our metrics for future use when our unconscious biases kick in or the biases of others intensify the team's emotional responses.

ZONE # 1: IDEAL

Picture yourself at Wimbledon watching a men's tennis tournament. The two players are wearing white and they use similar rackets. The court is clearly marked and a net stretches across it. The spectators sit quietly in the stands, happily sipping lemonade. The grass is green, the sun is shining, and the players perform with ease. All is well.

ZONE #2: OK

Let's move on to a Super Bowl football game. We're overlooking a huge field with the players suited up in uniforms, with different colors indicating opposing sides. The ball is oval and the net is stretched over the goal posts. The players slam into each other, and the crowd, eating hot dogs and drinking beer, yells and boos. The team manager argues loudly with the referee, who makes a bad call against our team. This isn't the best game we've ever attended, but we're still okay with it. But when it starts to rain, we look around and see some of the crowd is leaving. That's disorienting and maybe we should leave, too.

ZONE # 3: UPSET

Next, we're watching the reality show, *Survivor*, which the producers have set in the Amazon. Men and women are competing against each other. Not everyone is an athlete and they're wearing what looks like unwashed cast-offs. The action involves survival skills, including building a shelter, finding water, and gutting a fish. The rules seem random; we don't know who will get kicked off next. The players fight amongst themselves and one contestant contracts malaria. We're getting upset and wonder what we'll do if the show gets worse.

ZONE # 4: NIGHTMARE

Now picture a desert in the hottest time of day. At first, there's nothing to see but a few rocks and some tumbleweeds. Then, in the distance, you see a lone man slowly but determinedly make his way up a sand dune, only to find nothing but sand on the other side. He stumbles and tumbles down the dune, landing face down at the bottom. Several scorpions crawl out from under a boulder and bite him. You hear him scream and see him trying to crawl away from the scorpions. We watch his agony and feel his pain in this worst-case scenario. It's a nightmare and we can't leave fast enough.

PERSONAL BAROMETER WORKSHEETS

Each participant creates their personal barometer through storytelling to prepare themselves for team work in small groups. Here are worksheets to facilitate that creation, followed by examples of individual responses.

LEVEL #1 – IDEAL

1. Where are you and who are you with?

2. What season/weather is it?

3. What are you wearing?

4. What are you eating or drinking?

5. What music or sounds do you hear?

LEVEL #2 – OK

1. Where are you and who are you with?

2. What season/weather is it?

3. What are you wearing?

4. What are you eating or drinking?

5. What music or sounds do you hear?

LEVEL #3 – UPSET

1. Where are you and who are you with?

2. What season/weather is it?

3. What are you wearing?

4. What are you eating or drinking?

5. What music or sounds do you hear?

LEVEL #4 – NIGHTMARE

1. Where are you and who are you with?

2. What season/weather is it?

3. What are you wearing?

4. What are you eating or drinking?

5. What music or sounds do you hear?

SAMPLE RESPONSES

PARTICIPANT # 1

IDEAL: In the mountains with my wife, it's fall, I'm wearing a wool sweater, eating grilled seafood and listening to soft music.

OK: I'm in town in the summer wearing a white shirt and tie, eating a salad and listening to loud music.

UPSET: I'm in NYC in July in a three-piece suit eating fast food and surrounded by loud noise.

NIGHTMARE: I'm with people I hate in December in plaid pants eating fast food three times a day and listening to country music.

PARTICIPANT # 2

IDEAL: I'm on a grassy hill under a tree with my husband. It's spring and I'm wearing loose-fitting clothes, eating chocolate, and listening to country music.

OK: I'm in a boring lecture wearing an old suit and listening to the audience yawn.

UPSET: I'm someplace my loved ones don't like, wearing inappropriate clothes. I have only fast food to eat and hear too many loud voices.

NIGHTMARE: I'm lost in a crowd of strangers when I'm exhausted, wearing too-tight clothes. I'm hungry with only rotted food to eat and hear threatening voices.

PARTICIPANT # 3

IDEAL: I'm at a major league baseball game in the summer with my wife wearing shorts and a T-shirt eating Italian ice and listening to the game.

OK: I'm in a business meeting in late fall (end of daylight savings) eating donuts and trying to listen to the proceedings.

UPSET: I'm doing a business presentation on a spring day wearing a suit and tie drinking coffee and listening to myself drone on.

NIGHTMARE: I'm in court with strangers in the middle of winter wearing jail clothes, eating nothing and hearing lies.

WORKSHEET: Create the Team Story

Participants will enhance their decision-making skills by creating a team story that is based on four key concepts in the Conscious Choices Matrix: Avoid, Tolerate, Manage, and Impasse. We begin with having each participant fill out a simplified story worksheet before working in teams. When participants have completed the worksheets, they share their written stories out loud to the team of 3-6 participants. The team then creates a single group story based on the individuals' stories. Each team member keeps track of their personal Emotional Levels and Conscious Choices and will share their work with the team at the conclusion. The group appoints a team scribe to compile these notes and report on the process, along with the actual team story, to the larger group.

COMMUNICATION UN-BIAS MATRIX					
WHO	WHAT	WHEN	WHERE	WHY	SHORT HAND
Gender	Incident	Holy Day	Office	Faith	Movies
Race	Stale mate	Holiday	Street	Hope	TV
Ethnicity	Conflict	Night Time	Home	Equity	Music
Age	Clash	Daytime	Group	Kind	Food
Religion	Shun	Yearly	Class room	Facts	Art
Region	Insult	Monthly	Airport	Logic	Symbols
Socio-Economic	Mistake	Weekly	Store	Training	Names

LEVEL #1: IDEAL

- Where are you?

- What are you doing?

- Who are you with?

- What are you eating?

- What music/sounds do you hear?

LEVEL #2: OK

- Where are you?

- What are you doing?

- Who are you with?

- What are you eating?

- What music/sounds do you hear?

LEVEL #3: UPSET

- Where are you?

- What are you doing?

- Who are you with?

- What are you eating?

- What music/sounds do you hear?

LEVEL #4: PAINFUL

- Where are you?

- What are you doing?

- Who are you with?

- What are you eating?

- What music/sounds do you hear?

SAMPLE OF TEAM STORY

IDEAL: We're taking it easy at a place by the water with our partners listening to the silence and having a buffet.

OK: We're walking around a strange city with friends we've just met, listening to people in the street and drinking water.

UPSET: We're walking in really hot weather, listening to boring music and pesky buzzing insects with office people we don't like and there's nothing to eat.

NIGHTMARE: We're waiting in an airport with strangers in a hostile foreign country and shouted at in a language we don't understand with nothing but insects to eat.

SAMPLE OF TEAM CONSCIOUS CHOICES

AVOIDANCE: We all agreed not to deal with the issue of country music.

RESOLUTION: We resolved the issue of who would be with us by using the generic "partners" terminology.

MANAGE: We compromised about the sounds we heard overseas and chose something no one particularly liked but no one felt was too annoying.

IMPASSE: We had a heated discussion about where we would be in our ideal setting. There was no agreement or compromise between the athletes and the couch potatoes on the team. Finally, we agreed to break up the team.

CONCLUDING EXERCISE: CHECK YOUR TEAM WORK

The team has now shared their individual stories and created one team story together. This communal vision may have come easily to the group, but many times, it does not. Did the process result in a stable team, one that can go on to create, innovate, and work well together?

EMOTION UN-BIAS MATRIX - CONSCIOUS CHOICES-1-1			
AVOIDANCE +Plus -Minus	**RESOLUTION** +Plus -Minus	**MANAGE** +Plus -Minus	**IMPASSE** +Plus -Minus
+Buy time	+Agree to disagree	+Negotiate	-Run out of options
+Pick your battles	+Forgive & forget	+Get under control	-No common ground
-Bury it	-Just move on	-Manipulate	-Brought to a standstill
-Sweep under the rug	-Mistake to bring it up	-Endless back & forth	-No exit strategy

Team members can "check their work" and team status by asking each participant to describe their comfort level with the team choices in creating the group story. Each team member will choose either plus or minus in each of the first three categories according to their perception of the process. The answers will assess how much each person felt they had to compromise to create the team story. Compromise is a valuable tool when avoidance becomes too uncomfortable. If we cannot quickly resolve the issue, we try to manage the conflict and negotiate a compromise. Yet, if the compromise did not settle emotional issues and some team members felt they compromised too much, they might remain in the #3 Level.

If the responses tend to be Levels #1 or #2, then team communication and negotiation of conflict has been successful. However, if the team has participants who respond that they are in Level #3 with the final product, then the team needs to lower the emotion level, revisit the exercise and renegotiate.

Impasse is a definite possibility if emotions are at Level #4 when you check your teamwork. Whenever there is disagreement at this level, adrenaline kicks with the Fight or Flight response. There are several strategies that can be used to avoid Impasse for the team.

- Empathy: Allow the arguments to be heard respectfully and ask group for suggestions.

- Avoid: Buy time by suggesting a recess.

- Action: Decide to further investigate the problem.

- Plan: Design umbrella alternatives that are larger in scope and include more choices.

- Renegotiate and "check your work" at regular intervals using the Emotional Barometer.

- BREATHE! - See p. 59

SECTION 5: Wise Decision-making

"We're all biased, right, in many different ways - politically, religiously, ideologically, the way
our family raised us - and that's fine. Nobody wants to live in a world where everybody thinks
exactly the same. The key, though, is to try to figure out where your biases are holding you back
from solving problems."
~ Stephen J. Dubner

Wise decision-making began the structuring of information in the Culture Map and Communication Matrix. That first section teaches how to organize information, build a common language across personality and cultural boundaries, and develop organizational cultures while allowing for personal and group variations. Awareness of bias, unconscious and conscious, was embedded in the structuring process.

"Information is a source of learning. But unless it is organized, processed, and available to the
right people in a format for decision making, it is a burden, not a benefit."
~ William Pollard

When combined with the Emotion Matrix and the Wisdom Matrix, the first section's information and awareness become constructive planning tools for leaders and teams. The second section teaches emotional intelligence as we integrate our biases into sensitized teams able to manage their diversity.

The third section on Wisdom provides the tools for problem-solving and the leadership that leads to wise decisions. These decisions demonstrate the appropriate knowledge, accountability, and people skills; wise decisions upon which to plan, create, and innovate.

Decision-making in today's world is a challenge. There are decisions that need to be made immediately, others that can be delayed. Some require research and others are guided by emotion. Business decisions, personal decisions, and community decisions all have their own set of circumstances. When even one detail of timing, resources, or personality changes, then the choices also change. There is so much information and so many voices that it is easy to be overwhelmed and revert to our unconscious biases. How do we then recognize what is a wise decision in such a volatile environment? When workshop participants are asked to define a wise decision, the first response is generally silence. Even after a substantial pause, answers to "What is a wise decision?" are often tentative and very short. But the questions begin the conscious thinking process about how wise decisions are made.

Here are some typical answers:

- Fair
- Thoughtful
- Smart
- Reasonable
- Responsible
- Successful
- Profitable

When asked how they made these decisions, most participants were not conscious of how they made decisions. Typical answers included the following:

- Went with the flow
- Took my best guess
- Did the right thing
- Went with my gut
- Made a leap of faith
- Trusted the leadership
- Slept on it
- Tossed a coin
- Did what I could
- Did what worked the last time

These responses are virtually impossible to replicate, sustain, or teach. If their hunches worked, workshop participants described themselves as lucky, not wise. The inability to articulate how decisions were made meant a lack of consciousness that eventually affected team decisions.

"It's amazing how unwilling most people are to admit they don't know the answer to a question or a problem and instead charge forward on a 'gut instinct' that turns out to be crap."
~ Stephen J. Dubner (1963...)

Let's take an example of how difficulty in articulating the decision-making process can be a roadblock to success. Consider the phrase "do the right thing." Let's use a scenario in which one participant says to its team that the problem would be solved if they had "done the right thing." The group responds with confusion, frustration, defensiveness, and ultimately, resentment. Rather than rally to "do the right thing," the team feels unappreciated and they are angry that their character has been questioned.

What happened here? The participant and the team now are at an impasse and have a very high level of discomfort. The key factor here is that the phrase "do the right thing" addresses not the team's planning, action, or vision. Rather, it applies to the integrity, character, and reputation of the team. Answering that charge is virtually impossible and it is unlikely that this impasse will be resolved without tremendous effort. Too often, the response to impasse is not helpful:

- Participants may try to solve the problem before they define it.
- They tend to want a quick "magic bullet" solution.
- Participants may voice their negative emotions only at the end of the decision-making process, thereby distorting it.
- Overwhelmed participants may choose to absent themselves and avoid negotiations.

Could awareness of the undercurrents and sensitivity to the emotions in this situation have headed off this impasse? In this section, we examine the elements of wisdom and factor in the Character theme, early in the process of making wise decisions. As you go through the section, think of situations in your past or in your organization where wisdom might have improved the decisions. If you are able to master the decision-making process, you will see that it is a major asset for an organization.

BENEFITS OF WISE DECISION MAKING

- Better long-range planning
- More creative problem-solving
- More accurate anticipation of consequences
- Broader exchange of knowledge
- More diverse workplace/vendors/markets
- Less miscommunication across cultural boundaries
- Minimization of frustration and time wasted
- Attraction of quality human resources

THE WISDOM UN-BIAS MATRIX

The first step in making wise decisions is to organize the categories in which decisions are made so that conscious choices and plans can follow. This matrix is a flexible organizational structure that is a catalyst for connecting information and building new neuro pathways. The result is a decision-making and planning process that minimizes negative unconscious biases and their expression as intentional prejudice. The discussion scenarios in this section are intended to give workshop participants the opportunity to make conscious choices to improve situations where unconscious thinking led to unsatisfactory results.

WISDOM UN-BIAS MATRIX				
EXPERTISE	CHARACTER	HUMANITY	VISION	ACTION
Education	Committed	Kindness	Inspire	Plan
Information	Fairness	Empathy	Motivate	Delegate
Skills	Honesty	Caring	Hopeful	Mentor
Training	Trust	Make a Difference	Creative	Recruit
Experience	Accountable	Appreciate	Innovate	Promote
Research	Responsible	Nurture	Futurist	Reward

DISCUSSION SCENARIOS

1. EXPERTISE

Team A is struggling with a project whose deadline has been extended several times. They are waiting for Team B to complete its research, but Team B is also struggling with the new initiative. The project is a new initiative of the leadership of Organization X and cannot be completed using the organization's usual operating procedures.

What can they do to fix this?

2. CHARACTER

Team B is struggling with a project that provides new and different services to an on-going client and it cannot be completed using the usual processes of the organization. They were told to use the research provided by Team D. When Team B is unable to provide the research, Team A is told to complete the project without the Team B's research by the deadline promised to the client. The client is dissatisfied with the results and threatens to withdraw from on-going negotiations for future contracts with Organization X.

What could be done to fix this?

3. HUMANITY

In order to meet the client's deadline, Team C proceeded without the necessary research from Team D. Team C appeals to its leadership for project guidelines. Given that the project is unrelated to their usual services, leadership is unable to comply with the request and ask for creative solutions from Team C. The results are not what were promised to the client. The disappointed client refuses to pay for the services, given their inferior quality. The leadership makes up the lost revenue by firing half of the members of Team C.

What else could have been done to fix this?

4. VISION

The leadership of Organization X decided to diversify its projects and accepted a contract with a long-time client for services it didn't usually provide. Team D was given the responsibility of providing the research on the necessary components to complete the project to Team E. However, the project was only marginally related to the organization's mission. Team D did not have the appropriate expertise on staff and was not able to complete the research by the extended deadline. Team E proceeded without the research from Team D and met the deadline, but the results weren't relevant to the client's vision.

How could this have been handled better?

5. ACTION

Needing to cut costs, Organization X decides to fire half of its experts and not to offer all of the services it has provided in the past. A regular client now refuses to pay on current contracts or finalize negotiations for future contracts. Organization X decides to sue the client. When the client threatens a countersuit, leadership isn't sure what to do next.

EXERCISES

#1. What could Organization X done in the categories of EXPERTISE, CHARACTER, HUMANITY, VISION, and ACTION to lead to a positive result for the story's ending?

#2. Practice this wise decision-making process by taking your team story and turn the worst case scenario/NIGHTMARE into a best case scenario/IDEAL.
What EXPERTISE, CHARACTER, HUMANITY, VISION, and ACTION did you use?

SECTION 6: The Mission Un-Bias Matrix

You and your team are now ready to put your awareness, sensitivity, and competence into an action plan. Begin by defining your personal mission and goals for the workplace. Next, you'll apply that information and methodology in a team context. The result is a shared plan that benefits each team member, each team, and the organization.

STEP #1: VISION & MISSION WORKSHEET

Planning requires conscious thought, but it reflects unconscious thinking and biases. We can best make conscious choices by combining the COMMUNICATION, EMOTION, and WISDOM MATRICES. The first step is to articulate your Vision and your Mission. The Vision extends 10-20 years into the future while the Mission extends 5-9 years. Get started by defining your personal Vision and Mission. By doing this in writing rather than orally, you are encouraging your brain to connect and strengthen neuro-pathways. This is especially true when given a limited word count that forces you to condense the information.

Begin your planning process by writing in 25 words or less…

VISION: (10-20 years into the future)

MISSION: (5-9 years into the future)

STEP #2: GOAL WORKSHEET

List 3 goals related to your mission that you'd like to achieve in the next 1-4 years. Always begin by reviewing your mission. Next, list the goals using only 10 words each. Indicate whether you are passionate or just committed to achieving each goal. The process will add to your competence in making conscious choices.

YOUR MISSION:

GOAL #1:

Check one: ____Passionate   OR   ____ Committed

GOAL #2:

Check one: ____Passionate   OR   ____ Committed

GOAL #3:

Check one: ____Passionate   OR   ____ Committed

STEP #3: ASSETS MATRIX

Take stock of your personal assets for achieving these goals. Do that by filling in the following ASSETS matrix. List 4 items in each category and then rank the items 1-4. Grading yourself gives you additional awareness of your competence level.

1= Expert   2 = Good   3 = Needs improving   4 = Beginner

UN-BIAS MATRIX - Planning / Inventory

I KNOW	Rank 1-4	I VALUE	Rank 1-4	I'VE DONE	Rank 1-4	WITH WHOM? (clients/ audience)	Rank 1-4

TEAM PLANNING

Begin your team (3-8 members) planning exercise by choosing a scribe who begins the process by listing the goals from the personal worksheets and indicating 1) how many times the same goal was mentioned and 2) if a goal was ranked as "Passionate."

SCRIBE'S LIST OF GOALS

List individuals' goals, $\#$ of times the same goal was mentioned, and adding $+$ if Passionate.

    1

    2

    3

    4

    5

    6

    7

    8

    9

    10

    11

    12

    13

TEAM GOALS
VOTING

The team votes for the 3 goals that have been mentioned more than once and/or Passionate. Votes can either be for top priority (#1 = Ideal) or 2nd choice (#2 = OK). When there is disagreement, choose 3 goals that have a majority of the team rank as #1 with a minority of #2.

GOALS RANKED #1

GOALS RANKED #2

TEAM'S CHOICE OF GOALS TO PURSUE
1)
2)
3)

HUMAN CAPITAL ASSESSMENT

Many teams will have the assets and resources they need to pursue their goals within the team. Rather than assume this is the case, the team should discuss what human capital may be needed that's not listed in the individual worksheets. As a team, fill out the Planning / Needs worksheet and determine what assets should be added to the group.

UN-BIAS MATRIX - Planning / Needs				
GOALS	KNOWLEDGE	TRUST BUILDING	EXPERIENCE	WITH WHOM? clients/audience
GOAL #1				
GOAL #2				
GOAL #3				

DISCUSSION QUESTIONS

Conclude the planning process by discussing within your teams the possible biases that might interfere with achieving its goals. Divide those biases into 2 categories that are applied to both individuals and organizations.

CATEGORY #1: Intentional/ Conscious Bias

Individual: What preferences do your team members have that will either boost or limit the team's progress?

Organization: What rules and regulations require bans or limits, such as bathroom policies, that may influence the results of your team's efforts?

CATEGORY #2: Unconscious Bias

Individual: Do team members have an emotional response to specific issues or target populations that limits the collaboration of the team?

Organization: Are there policies in place that result in discrimination, although they do not appear to do so on the surface, including language and physical strength requirements?

BREATHE!

There will be moments in the process of Un-Bias when you may feel anxious, highly emotional, and confused. Take a break, give yourself time to digest new information, make new neuro-pathway connections, and re-define yourself, your goals, and your team. Before you go to work, do this breathing exercise. Repeat at least two times a day for three weeks and when confronted with a stressful situation. The habit of breathing to counteract stress will then be established as part of your toolbox for making conscious choices.

BREATHING EXERCISE

- Sit quietly and close your eyes.
- Inhale through your nose and take a deep breath beginning with your belly, then your rib cage, and followed by your upper chest.
- Slowly exhale and begin to count down from 10 out loud.
- REPEAT for 9, 8, 7, 6, 5, and 4. When you get to 3, say it three times as you exhale (3, 3, 3). Do the same for 2 and 1.
- When you're finished counting, take a few quiet breaths, open your eyes, and move forward into your day.

"Take a shower, wash off the day. Drink a glass of water. Make the room dark. Lie down and close your eyes. Notice the silence. Notice your heart. Still beating. Still fighting. You made it, after all. You made it, another day. And you can make it one more. You're doing just fine."
~ *Charlotte Eriksson*

"Being under stress is like being stranded in a body of water. If you panic, it will cause you to flail around so that the water rushes into your lungs and creates further distress. Yet, by calmly collecting yourself and using controlled breathing you remain afloat with ease."
~ *Alaric Hutchinson*

"When life is foggy, path is unclear and mind is dull, remember your breath. It has the power to give you the peace. It has the power to resolve the unsolved equations of life …Conscious breathing is the best antidote to stress, anxiety and depression."

~ Amit Ray

"With every breath, the old moment is lost; a new moment arrives. We exhale and we let go of the old moment. It is lost to us. In doing so, we let go of the person we used to be. We inhale and breathe in the moment that is becoming. In doing so, we welcome the person we are becoming. We repeat the process. This is meditation. This is renewal. This is life."

~ Lama Surya Das

About The Author

DEBORAH J. LEVINE is an award-winning author of twelve books on cultural diversity, Editor-in-Chief of the *American Diversity Report,* and a newspaper Op-Ed columnist. Deborah designs creative resources such as the *Matrix Model Management System, Inspire your Inner Global Leader: True Stories for New Leaders,* and *Religious Diversity at Work: Guide to Religious Diversity in the US Workplace.* She has won a National Press Association Award, been featured on CSPAN-BOOKTV, and was named a Finalist in the national 2017 Indie Book competition.

Deborah has provided workshops, presentations, and coaching to government agencies, nonprofits, universities, and corporations. The government agencies include the US National Park System, TN Office of Diversity & Small Business, Chattanooga Department of Education, Arts & Culture, Chicago North River Agency. The nonprofits include BlueCross BlueShield of TN, Birmingham International Center, Unity Huntsville, Allied Arts/Chattanooga, Jewish Federations of America. Universities include the University of Tennessee at Chattanooga, University of Alabama Medical College, Auburn University, Elmhurst College, Southern Adventist University, William Andrews Clark Library/UCLA, and the National Association of Veterinarian Colleges. Her corporate clients include: Volkswagen, Nissan, International Paper, Siemens.

She has advanced degrees in cultural anthropology and urban planning, attending Harvard University, New York University, Spertus Institute of Jewish Studies, and the University of Il. at Chicago. She served as Research Coordinator of the College of Engineering & Computer Science/ University of TN at Chattanooga.

Brought up in the British commonwealth of Bermuda, Deborah has lived, worked, and studied in multiple states across the US and is currently headquartered in Tennessee.

Her leadership includes founding the Southeast Women's Council on Diversity, The DuPage/Chicago Interfaith Resource Network, and the Chattanooga Global Leadership Class. She received awards from the TN Economic Council on Women, Girls Inc./Chattanooga, and the American Planning Association/Chicago.

Made in the USA
Middletown, DE
10 August 2019